NEEDLEFELTING MAGIC

Making Beautiful
Teddybears

Diagrams and Photographs by Barbara Allen

Cobweb Cottage

Published by Cobweb Cottage
New Zealand

Diagrams and Photographs by Barbara Allen

First published 2003
Second impression 2007
Third impression 2010

ISBN 978-0-476-00196-1

Cover Design & Layout
by Tristan Brehaut for WillsonScott Publishing Ltd.
design@willsonscott.biz

Printed by Arrow Printing (2010) Ltd.

Contents

Introduction   5

PART ONE – A Basic Needlefelted Teddybear   7
Equipment   7
Making Your First Teddybear   11
Head   12
Ears   17
Nose   19
Eyes   20
Body   22
Attaching The Head   25
Legs   27
Arms   30

PART TWO – Advanced Techniques   33
Trimming   33
Adding Pawpads   34
Thread Claws   35
Curled Over Toes   36
Adding Toe Pads   37
Sharp Right-Angle Heel   38
Individual Toes and Fingers   39
Dropped Paws   40
Sideways Paws   41
Shaped Body   42
Tummy   43
Thread Eyebrows   44
Adding Thick Eyebrows or Jowls   45
Shading   46
Forming A Separate Muzzle   47
Adding An Open Mouth   48
Making A Panda   50
Accessories   53

Needlefelting Supplies   54
Summary   55
About The Author   56

Introduction

Needlefelting is an exciting new craft that is sweeping the world. It is achieved by poking wool roving or wool sliver with a special barbed needle many times until it begins to felt together. As you poke you are able to turn and shape the wool to form a teddybear head or arm, or any 3-dimensional shape you want. The finished piece is firm, not squashy, and is made of felted wool all the way through, so there is no stuffing needed and no stitching together either. Even the ears can be felted on, not stitched.

Commercial needlefelting has been around for more than a hundred years, making flat felt with machines by using beds of thousands of felting needles at a time. But it is only relatively recently that people have picked up just one of these felting needles and used them to create exquisite 3-dimensional sculptures by hand.

The degree of difficulty in the work is entirely up to the individual, and you can produce very nice teddies or other animals in a few hours, or spend many hours on a piece and take it to a very high level of art.

Needlefelting is a wonderful handcraft as it is inexpensive to get started and does not require any great skill, so is suitable for beginners as well as advanced craftspeople.

When I first heard of needlefelting I could not understand how it could possibly work. I was told that you "poke a special needle into the loose wool fibres and it will gradually mat up to form a ball". How could that be, when there was no thread on the end of the needle? So I ordered some needles, acquired a small amount of wool and started off. I was so amazed to find that it worked! Just like I had been told! And I loved it; needlefelting is so much fun, and very relaxing as you work your piece into shape.

Needlefelting is a dry felting process which, unlike traditional felt making, does not involve using soap and water. So needlefelting is clean, and very simple, with the minimum of equipment needed.

I have found that although there are some needlefelting books available, most of them do not go into much detail dealing specifically with teddybears, and how to achieve a high quality in your bears. I feel this is an area that deserves to be covered, as so many people enjoy making bears, so I have endeavoured to set out my own needlefelting ideas and experiences in this book.

In **Part One** I will teach you how to make your first needlefelted teddybear, and in **Part Two** I will discuss more advanced techniques and tips to encourage you to experiment with this exciting craft. I have written this book so that it will appeal to both experienced bear makers and also craftspeople who have never made a teddybear before.

I suggest you read through the entire book thoroughly first to get a general overview, and then go back to the beginning and work your way through the instructions.

Enjoy yourself !

PART ONE: A Basic Needlefelted Teddybear

Equipment

In order to begin needlefelting, you will need several felting needles, some wool roving or sliver and a small block of foam rubber as a work surface.

Felting Needles

A felting needle has no 'eye' at the end, just a small handle turned at right angles to the main shaft. The shaft is generally about 9 cm (3.5 inches) long, and the lower part of the shaft has tiny barbs on it. These barbs hook onto the fibres as you poke the needle in to the wad of wool, entangling them deeply with the other fibres. Gradually as you work the wool becomes matted and felted.

Felting needles come in many different varieties. They may have a triangular shaped shaft or a star shaped shaft, both with the tiny barbs arranged around the edges and pointing downwards. There are numerous other types of shaft available for specialist work, but for our purposes we will begin with the triangle and star shape.

The triangle (T) shaped shafts are used most of the time and have a three-sided shaft with barbs on each edge.

The star (S) needles have four-sided shafts. Each side scoops inwards to make the 'star' shape, so the hole that is left in the work is much smaller than that left by the triangle shaft. This means that the star needle can be used for much finer detailing work.

Some needles have the barbs spread several centimetres up the shaft (eg. #36T), and others have them clustered closer to the tip (eg. #40S) or in differing arrangements along the shaft. The needles with barbs closer to the tip are used for the finer detailed work and the longer shaft needles are used at the beginning of the project, when you have a relatively large, loose mass of wool and want to felt it down quickly into a more manageable size.

As the felting needles are very sharp, you must be careful not to poke your fingers with them. They are also brittle, and will break - not bend - if you force them on an angle. However, if properly used, a needle will last for a very long time. When I first started I broke a few needles, through inexperience. Now I very rarely break one, and they are not expensive if you have to buy another needle anyway. It is a good idea to have a few spare needles on hand for just such an emergency.

The most common sizes used in fine needlefelting are:
#36T (triangle)
#38T
#38S (star)

#40T
#40S
#42T

The larger the number, the finer the needle, so #36 is coarser than #40. I mainly use three sizes in my work; #36T, #40T, and then #40S for fine detailing at the end.

Felting needles are not expensive, so for a relatively low cost you can keep a variety of sizes for your work. The #36T is readily available in needlework shops, but this seems to be the only size they have. Other sizes are harder to find, but you should be able to buy them from a felting supply shop. I keep a range of needle sizes for sale if you are having difficulty locating them.

I like to keep my needles safe in a plastic container. You can buy a variety of long thin containers for your needles. I find that an old plastic spice container is perfect, with a thin piece of foam pushed in to the bottom of it to protect the needle tips as you drop them in. To identify which needle is what size, you may find it helpful to paint different coloured nail varnish on the handles of the different sizes, as it can be difficult to tell, just by looking, without a magnifying glass.

Wool Roving Or Sliver

This is what the spinners use when spinning their wool. It is readily available in a range of colours, and is ideal to use for needlefelting.

I find NZ corriedale wool felts up beautifully and is what I use most of the time; merino is very fine and because of this can take a little longer to felt, but it is still very nice to work with. There is a whole range of other fibres out there that can be used (eg. alpaca or camel's wool) and you may find it fun to experiment with them to see what they are like.

Wool comes in natural colours, as well as beautiful brightly dyed colours if you want to make a very colourful project or perhaps need a small amount of contrast in your piece.

You may already have fibre of your own that you can use to needle felt, or you can buy small bags of wool for only a few dollars each.

A Foam Block

This is used as a work base, to rest your wool on and poke the needle into. I find foam is very good, as it doesn't seem to blunt the needles (polystyrene blocks tend to blunt the needles). The foam also forms a good protective barrier between your knee and the sharp needle. When you pause in your work, you can poke the needle in to the foam to keep it from getting lost.

That is all you need to get started.

Making Your First Teddybear

For those of you who have not made a teddybear before, using the conventional method of sewing fur-type fabric together, I have included here a diagram of the basic teddy shapes that I will be referring to in this book. (Fig.1)

Use the shapes as a guide only, as everybody will find that their bears grow into individuals as they work, and they may turn out quite different to how you envisage them in the first place. I find this happens to me a lot, when I am making a bear with a certain 'look' in mind. By the time I have finished the bear may have developed completely differently, but he still looks really cute!

It is not possible to make a proper pattern for a felted bear, so each bear is a real individual, although it is possible to follow a diagram or pictures to make a similar bear to what you see.

The bears I make range from about 6.5cm (2 inches) tall, when standing, to about 10cm (4 inches). I prefer not to make them too much larger as it will take much longer to felt, so for your first bear, try not to make him too big.

Here you will see the suggested shapes for the teddy head, body, arms and legs. The smaller shape is the ear, with some wispy fibres hanging down from it to use to attach to the head.

There is almost no sewing in a needlefelted bear. The only time you use an ordinary needle is to embroider the nose, and attach the limbs and the eyes.

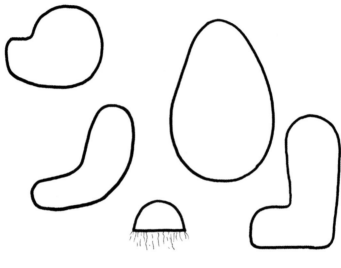

Fig.1

We will begin with the head, as I use this, once it is finished, to gauge the size of the body and limbs that will be needed.

The Head

To begin, take your #36T needle, and pull off a smallish wad of wool from your roving. I like to pull off several small pieces, rather than one large piece, and then I pull it apart and mix it a little with my fingers so that the fibres are not all lying in the same direction, but are mixed up in all directions.

To try to gauge how small your wad of wool will be when you have finished felting it (i.e. the size of the finished teddy head), try to scrunch it up into the tightest ball you can in your hands, and that will give you a rough idea.

Now open up the wad of wool again so that it is quite loose, and place it on your foam pad (I like to work with the foam on my knee, but you may prefer to work with it on the table). Take your felting needle and poke it down through the loose wool until you feel it poke into the foam, then lift it directly out again. That is all it takes!

Now you are felting!

Poke your wool about 4 to 6 times, and at this stage each poke needs to be spaced well apart, about 2 cm (3/4 inch) away from the previous one. Then pick the wad up off the foam and turn it over about a quarter turn and poke it again about 4 to 6 times. Later on as the piece works down you will gradually be able to bring your poke points closer and closer. But at this stage, keep them well apart. Keep poking and turning, poking and turning, and you will soon see it is beginning to hold its shape and become felted. BUT do be aware of where your fingers are all the time so that you don't prick yourself (this will soon become automatic as you get more experienced). You will find that each time you pick up your wool to turn it, there will be some fibres embedded in the foam, but these will pull out with the wad of wool each time you pick it up. This is a normal part of needlefelting.

Tip: At this early stage, before the wool has formed any shape, it is important not to poke more than 4 to 6 times into one area before turning, or you will very quickly have a piece of flattened felt in front of you, which you do NOT want. Keep on TURNING it as you felt, so that you develop a rounded shape. I cannot emphasise this enough, as once you have flattened the felt too much it is very difficult to make a three-dimensional shape.

Make sure at this stage that you are poking your felting needle deeply right through the wad of wool, and slightly into the foam block. This will ensure that the work is felted firmly all the way through. If you merely give it short, shallow pokes, just on the surface, you will find that the surface mats up but the inside will stay soft, and we don't want that. So long, deep pokes are needed at this early stage.

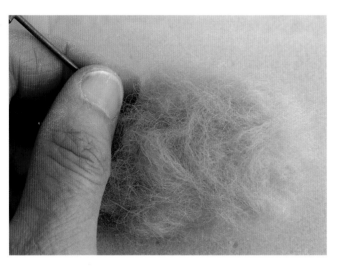

Now as you continue felting, you need to try to form the shape of an egg or oval. Remember as you form the oval, to keep paying attention to the ends, as well as the middle, or your piece will become too elongated. The ends of the oval will need just as much poking as the middle. You will find that if there is an area where the wool is bulging out too far, a few pokes with the felting needle will soon have it back in shape.

If you are developing flat areas with sharp edges, stop felting the flat areas for now, and poke at the sharp edges until they have been reduced to a more rounded shape. The reason that the flat edges have developed is because the needle has been poked too often into the same area without turning the work to a new area. If an area is poked repeatedly, it will go 'inwards', while the areas around it are being neglected and will appear to bulge out as unwanted lumps, so keep turning and poking, turning and poking, evenly all over.

When your shape is beginning to feel about half-firm and is a definite oval shape, you can change your needle to a #38 or #40, and start to apply more individual shaping. If you find at this stage that the surface appears to be rather bumpy, don't worry about it, just remember to poke the little bumps and avoid poking the hollows too much and the surface will eventually even out. You will find now that you can poke 8 to 12 times in an area before turning, as the head has developed and can hold its initial shape. The number of pokes before you turn is up to you at this stage, depending on how you are trying to shape an area.

Now you want to look at your head and decide which end of the oval is to be the nose, and try to make that end a little finer and more pointed than the other end which will be the back of the head. About halfway up your oval is where the eyes of the bear will eventually go. So keep these areas in mind as you continue needlefelting, trying to refine the shape more now. It is very important that the nose is felted firmly, as you are going to stitch the nose with thread later and you need a firm base in which to work.

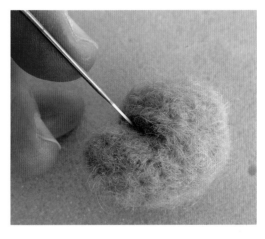

Before the head gets really hard, you need to begin shaping the forehead. To give the bear a distinct forehead make a line of pokes right across the top of the muzzle, just at or below where you intend the eyes to go. You will have to work on this dent and the areas above and below it for a while to get the shaping that you desire. I think a bear looks really cute when the nose is on a different angle to the forehead.

Tip: when you want a dent, or inwards bend, in your work, poke your needle repeatedly into that area for a while, and it will start to go inwards, eg. forehead, elbows, etc.

Now that you have the dent in place, keep working all around the head firming it up, but you will have to keep coming back to the forehead indent and re-working it to keep the definition there as the other areas are gradually felted down around it. As you work, keep testing the firmness with your fingers and if you find an area that is softer than elsewhere, work gently on that for a while until it firms up.

Tip: The degree of firmness varies with each individual's preference. When I first started my felted bears were softer, but now I prefer to felt them really hard, so that when I push on them there is almost no denting possible.

When you feel that the bear's head is as firmly felted, all over, as you can get it, and is a nice teddy shape, choose the position for the two eyes. I generally put a pin with a small head into each eye position, and that helps me to judge better whether the eye positions are even, and if they are where I want them to be.

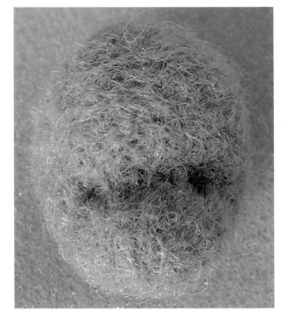

Now take out one of the pins and poke that small area repeatedly with your needle until you have a small indent there for the eye to rest in. Then do the same with the other eye. The #40 needle is ideal for this fine shaping.

The Ears

You need to make a half circle, flat shape for each ear, leaving some wispy bits of wool (only a tiny bit) at the bottom of the ear. These wispy bits will be used to attach the ear to the head. Because the ears are so small and flat, it is a good idea to work them with your #38 or #40 needle.

Pull off two tiny pieces of wool, the same size, for your two ears. You will not need much at all for each ear. Start off forming a rough ball shape with one of the pieces of wool, using your felting needle, and when it is starting to hold together, begin flattening the shape by poking on one side a few times, then turning the piece completely over and poking the other side. This is one of those times when you really do want to form a flat piece of

felt. To make the rounded upper edge of the ear, try to gently lift, with your needle, a few fibres that are sticking out over the edge, pull them over and felt them down in to the body of the ear. Work right around the upper edge like this, remembering to leave some wispy wool at the lower edge. Now turn the work over and repeat for the other side.

Tip: *At this stage you just need shallow pokes so that you are only just penetrating the foam. If you go too deeply you will find that there are lots of wispy bits of wool poking out the other side of your ear, each time you turn it over, and you don't really want that.*

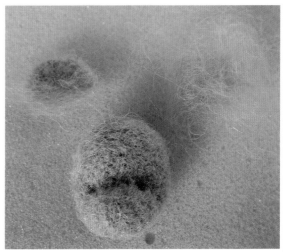

When your ear is holding its shape nicely and feels firm, but still a little bit larger than you want it to be when finished, you are ready to attach it to your bear's head.

Position one corner of the ear near the top of the head, about halfway between the nose tip and the back of the head. Holding the ear in place with one hand, carefully poke the needle down through the ear corner and deeply into the head. This will take the loose fibres from the ear and mat them down firmly in the felt of the head. You will need to poke the corner quite a few times until you feel it is holding.

Then position the lower corner of the ear where you want it and felt that into position until it is just holding. Now you can let go the ear with your other hand, and carefully poke down right around the back edge of the ear, and a little at the front, paying particular attention to making sure the corners are firmly felted on. We don't want the ears to be too floppy or loose, or they may get accidentally pulled off later on, so continue felting around for quite some time until you are satisfied that it feels very firmly attached, and the ear is about the size that you want it.

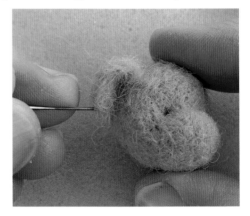

Then felt the other ear on, making sure that it looks even in size and position with the first ear. You may have to work for a while to get both ears looking the same. If you feel that one of the ears appears bigger than the other, poke your needle down through the ear, starting at the top edge and poking through the entire ear and into the head. If you do this a few times you will notice that the ear becomes smaller, but don't make it too small. Keep checking the size with the other ear as you work.

The Nose

The nose is embroidered using size 12 embroidery thread, or size 8 if you prefer. As you will not be able to bury a knot into the felt and hide it, the thread needs to be anchored in the head by passing it backwards and forwards about three times, always being careful to go back into the same hole that your thread came out of, and pulling so that it disappears, otherwise you may end up with a few tiny dark 'freckles' on your bear!

When your thread is anchored, make a horizontal guideline stitch across the top of where you want the nose to be, and a lower nose guideline stitch too, if it is going to be a rectangular nose, then embroider the nose using vertical satin stitch. (Fig.2) It is best to make the first vertical stitch in the middle of the nose, and then work out to one side. When you have finished that side, come back to the middle of the nose again and work out to the other side.

The nose will be more even if you do it this way. You will see now why it is important to firmly felt the nose area, so that it is easy to stitch.

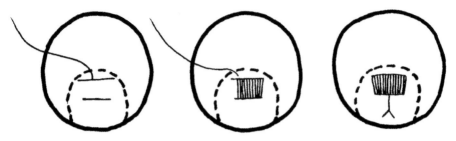

Fig.2

You may prefer to do a triangular nose shape, in which case you will only need to make a guide stitch across the top of the nose, working the lower stitches to a point at the bottom of the nose.

When the nose is finished (and the guide stitches covered), take the thread down below the nose and stitch an inverted Y shape for the mouth. Your head will be starting to look like a teddy now, all he needs is his eyes.

The Eyes

You can use round black beads for eyes, or conventional glass teddy eyes that have a wire loop at the back. I will describe using the glass eyes, as that is what I normally use myself.

Use a half hitch knot to attach a 38 cm (15 inch) length of dental floss folded in half, to the wire loop. Once the floss is attached you will need to squeeze the wire loop closed, using small pliers, so that the wire can be pulled down into the head and the eyes are held tight against the eye sockets that you have made. (Fig.3)

Thread both ends of floss from one eye on to a long needle, insert the needle in an eye socket and come out at the bottom of the head where the neck will be and leave the thread hanging loose there. Now do the same for the other eye, coming out about 0.5 cm (1/4 inch) away from the first thread. Pull both threads to firmly embed the eyes. When you are happy with the eye positions, tie the ends together tightly and leave them there at the neck (fig.4). These ends will be used later to attach the head to the body.

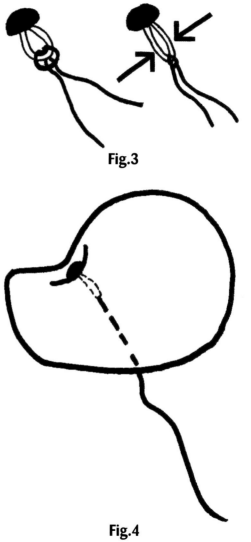

Fig.3

Fig.4

Now your bear's head is complete! This is the most exciting moment for me; when the eyes are in, the teddy's personality is starting to shine!

The Body

The body for a basic bear is also an oval, but I prefer to make the neck end a little more pointy and the lower end rather fatter, like an egg shape, so that teddy doesn't look too skinny (see the basic shapes diagram, fig.1). It also needs to be at least twice the size of the head you have made.

Once again, pull off several small pieces of wool and mix them slightly so that the fibres don't all lie in the same direction. You will need to begin with a larger wad than you did for the head.

Begin felting again, starting with your larger needle, poking and turning, poking and turning, until your wad is beginning to take shape. At first you should shape the wool into a round ball and work this down until you feel that

the diameter of the ball is just a little bigger than the length you want the body to be when it is completed. Now begin shaping the ball into an oval, by working the sides more than the ends. Change to your smaller needle when you feel ready to, and continue to work your piece down to a firm, egg shaped oval. The body does not need so much refinement as the head, so although it is slightly larger, it should be quicker to felt.

Remember to felt very firmly, so that the final shape will dent only very **slightly** when you squeeze it, but will bounce straight out again when you let go. I think firm felting is the sign of a good quality piece. Keep checking the piece all over for soft spots, and work these until they feel the same as the surrounding areas. The ends of the oval need to be just as firm as the sides, so they will need some care in working them down too.

You may find as you work down, that the body is going to be too small for the head size. In this case, you simply pull off some more wool, mix it slightly again in your fingers, then wrap it around the body where you want more volume, and needlefelt it on until it is as firmly felted as the original piece of the body. Take care to felt the bulk of the additional wool on the particular area that you want it, by coaxing and poking mainly in that area,

or you may find that it has spread out all over the body and not stayed where you intended it to be. Feather out the edges of the wool as you felt it, to make sure that you don't leave any obvious join lines where the first and second pieces of wool meet.

This method is also good if you find that you have a hollow area somewhere that you just can't get rid of. Take a little more wool and lay it over the hollow, felting it down until it is as firm as the rest of the piece, and feathering out the edges as above so that they don't show.

This is one of the joys of working with needlefelting. It is a very forgiving medium and you can increase or decrease the size of the piece very easily.

If you find that the body is far too large or long, by the time that you have felted it down as hard as you can, then use your scissors, or a knife, to cut or trim it down to the required size. Then take a small wisp of wool roving and felt it over the cut edges to form a thin layer that will hide the cut, and you will never know that it is there. I have used this method several times to rescue a piece; it works wonderfully. Once I was working on an arm, and it became obvious that it was going to be far too fat, so I took the scissors

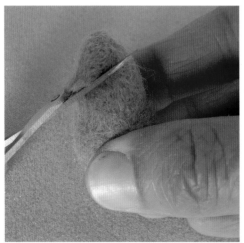 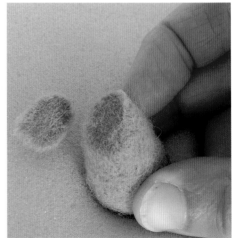

to it and snipped right down the centre of the arm, and formed both arms from the original piece.

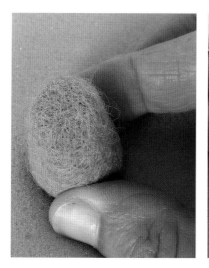 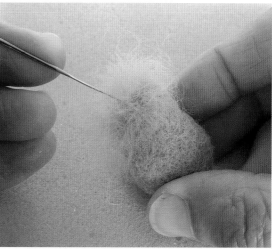

Attaching The Head To The Body

When your body is ready, you need to attach the head to it (fig.5). Take one of the double threads that you have left hanging under the neck of the head from inserting the eyes, and thread it on to a long needle (one that is longer than the length of your body). Insert the needle at the neck end of the body and take it straight down through the body and out at the lower end. Pull the thread all the way through.

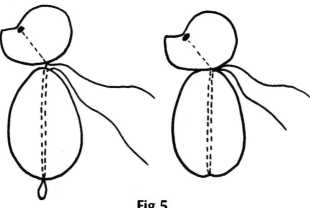

Fig.5

Now insert your needle back in the same hole as you just came out of and take it back up through the body to exit at the top, just 0.5 cm (1/4 inch) away from where you first inserted the needle. The idea is that you want the thread to disappear back inside the body at the lower end, but to grab some of the felt inside the body to hold on to when you pull tight.

Take the needle off and tie a knot with the remaining double thread from the other eye. You need to pull this very tight before you tie off the knot, so that the head is set firmly against the body, and not flopping around.

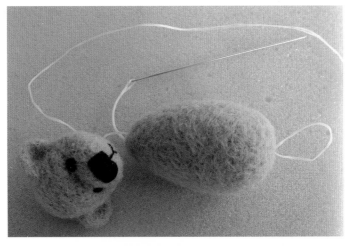

I prefer to use dental floss for jointing because the wax on the floss prevents it from slipping and coming loose when you are tying a knot.

When you are satisfied that the head is tied firmly, thread the ends on to your needle and take them down into the body, pull them tight, then cut them so

that they disappear back into the body. DON'T simply cut them off at the neck edge, or the knot may work itself loose and undo.

If you notice that a dimple has developed at the bottom of the body when you pulled your threads tight, don't worry about it, we can fix that up. Take a very tiny piece of loose wool, gently felt it on your foam block until it is starting to hold a bit of shape, then felt it on to the dimple with your felting needle, poking carefully so that you get the wool to fill in the indent and the

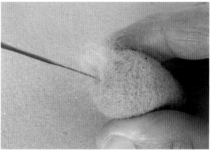

edges are feathered out so that they don't show the join. Work the area until it is felted to the same stage as the surrounding wool. That is how simple it

is to get rid of a dimple that may appear when you thread joint your bear.

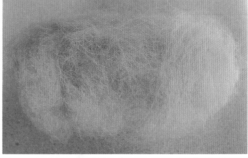

The Legs
To make the legs, we want to make a longish cylinder shape with the foot turned up at right angles at the end. Pull off two wads of wool and try to match them for size. These will be your two legs. The volume you will need for each leg will be perhaps half the volume of wool that you

needed for the body. It is easier to match up the amounts of wool for each leg now, rather than making one leg completely, then trying to remember how much you used when it comes to making the other leg.

Put one wad aside while you work on the first leg. As you did before, mix the wool with your fingers so that the fibres don't all lie in one direction. Now form a rough, loose cylinder shape and begin to felt it with your #36 needle. Remember to keep turning to prevent the work flattening out. Work along about two-thirds of the length, leaving the last third loose (this will be used to form the foot later). Change to a smaller needle as your work becomes firmer, and don't forget to work on the end that will become the hip joint, as this needs to be a very firmly felted area, so that you can thread joint in there later.

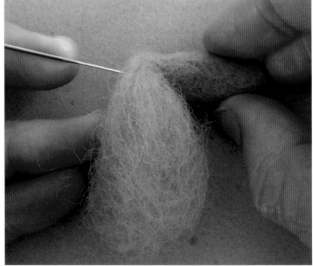

When the leg has felted down to the firmness that you require, you are ready to turn the foot. Place the leg upside down and bend the loose fluffy threads at right angles to the leg and needlefelt from the heel back down into the length of the leg. This will give you a good bend for the foot. Now turn your work back up the right way and needlefelt the foot into shape. Poke all around, including from the toes area back towards the heel, making sure that you are not flattening it out too much. Keep turning your work, and don't forget to work into the heel area some more to firm that up too. In order to work comfortably on the underneath of the foot, you may find it helpful to turn the leg upside down and drop the leg part over the edge of the foam, leaving the foot on the foam to work with.

Repeat with the wool for the other leg, keeping the first leg beside you so that you can refer back to it often to try to make them the same shape.

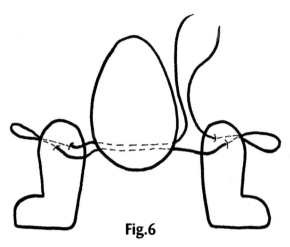

Fig.6

Before you joint the legs to the body, check one more time on the firmness of the top of the legs to see that they are not soft. If they are, work on them some more, until they are firm.

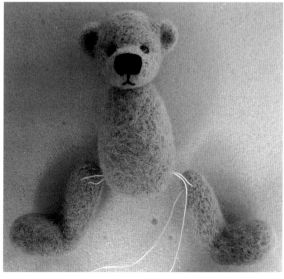

Now we are ready to join the legs onto the body (fig.6). Take a length of dental floss about 38 cm (15 inches) and thread it on to your long needle, just a single thread. Insert the needle near the top of your first leg, on the inside of the leg, and take it out the other side, leaving a length of thread hanging out at the beginning that you can use to tie a knot later. Now go straight back in the same hole as you came out of and come out beside your first thread, about 0.3 cm (1/8 inch) away. This will allow the dental floss to grab some of the wool in the leg but hide the dental floss stitch from the outside leg. Sit the bear's body on the table, and place the leg against the body so that it is going to be in a nice position when the bear is sitting down. Work out where the needle needs to be inserted in the body to keep that position, and go right through the body and out the other side, keeping the needle level, so that the legs stay the same height.

Take the needle through the other leg, from the inside to the outside, then back in the same hole and out 0.4 cm (1/8 inch) away.

Now take the needle back through the body and come out close to where it went in. Tie a knot using the thread that is hanging out of the first leg and the thread from the body, pulling the legs in very tightly so that they fit snugly against the body, and are not floppy. Then take each thread back through the body, pull tight and cut off so that they don't show.

The Arms

Now you are ready to make the arms. Pull off two even size wads of wool, one for each arm, making them slightly smaller than the wads you used for the legs. Mix the first wad with your fingers, then form a rough cylinder shape as for the legs. This time it will be simpler because there will be no foot, just a cylinder shape, bent slightly in the middle for the elbow. Work the arm down with

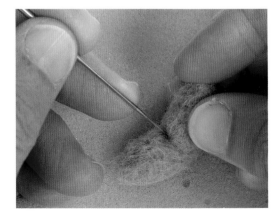

your large felting needle first, and change to the smaller needle when you feel ready. Work along the length of the whole arm, paying attention to both ends, as the paws and the shoulders need to be firm, not wispy. When it is about half-felted, begin making a bend for the elbow, about halfway along the arm, by poking repeatedly into one side until it begins to form a dent, and then continuing to work around the whole arm, and the sides and back of the elbow too. Work it down to a nice firmness, as you have done with the rest of the bear, and then make the other arm the same.

Join the two arms on to the body in the same way as you did the legs, but this time you need to decide how far down from the head that you want to place the arms. If they are very high up, your teddy will look like he is shrugging his shoulders; if you put them a bit lower down he will look more relaxed (fig.7). It really depends on what look you prefer. To try the positions out, put a pin through the arm 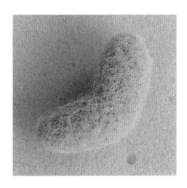 at the shoulder and pin it to the body, that will give you an idea of what he will look like.

Remember to pull the threads very tight when knotting them, so that the arms don't hang loosely, and then lose the ends back inside the body before cutting off.

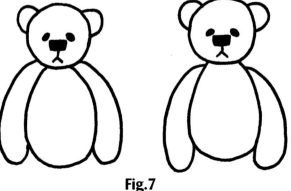

Fig.7

If you find that you have a dimple on the arm or leg where it has been jointed, repeat the process as for a dimple at the bottom of the body, joining a tiny piece of wool on and felting it firming to hide the dimple. You will need to use your smaller needle for this.

And now your teddy is complete. I am sure he looks very cute!

PART TWO

Advanced Techniques

Now we come to the part where you can add your own individual touches to enhance your creations. Here I have given instructions on many of the techniques I use on my bears, and I have a great deal of fun doing them.

You may find after you have worked through these, that you develop other ideas of your own, and that will be wonderful if you do; needlefelting, being such a new art, is growing and developing all the time, as people bring their own knowledge and ideas into the craft.

Trimming

When you have finished your piece, you may feel that there are too many stray fibres sticking out the sides. Some people like the look of these fibres and others don't. If you are not happy with them, you can very carefully trim them off with sharp scissors, and your bear will have a cleaner, more refined look. But be careful not to cut into the felt accidentally.

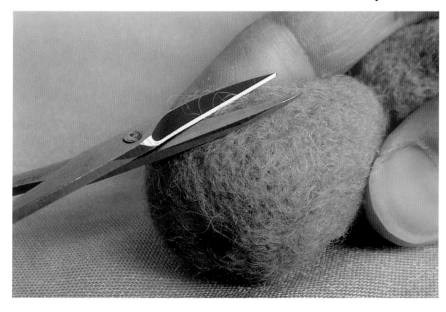

Adding pawpads

If you would like your bear to have pawpads of a different colour, then you can make them by adding a layer of another colour wool after you have finished needlefelting the arms and legs.

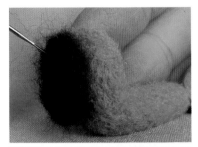

Take a small wad of wool in your chosen contrast colour, and felt it down gently on your foam block, turning it often, until you have a flat oval of felt that is about 3/4 felted. Now place it over the bottom of your foot and needlefelt it on, with your small needle.

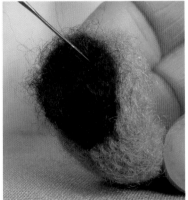

Make sure you don't poke too deeply through the foot, or the wisps of colour may come out on the top of the foot. You need to poke as deeply as you can, without coming out the top of the foot. Attach the middle first, then work around where you want the edges to be, pulling in the odd stray fibre with your needle, to make a neat edge. Make sure the pad is attached very firmly, so that it doesn't come off. Repeat for the pawpads on the arms, but make them smaller than the footpads.

Thread Claws

At this stage, if you want to you can add thread claws. Take a length of your nose thread with no knot in the end. Pass it through the paw several times to anchor it, then stitch on your claws where you want them to be (fig.8). You can stitch up to five claws, depending on your preference. Finish off by passing the thread several times through the foot again, to anchor it.

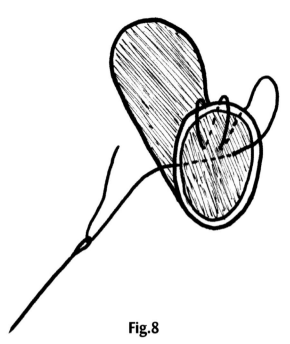

Fig.8

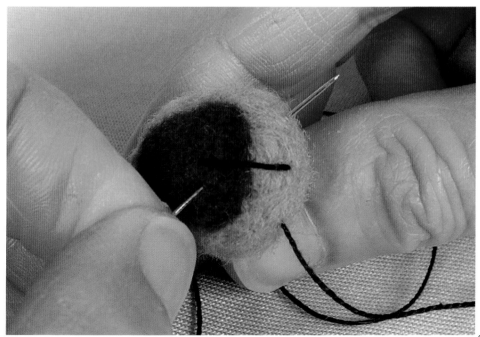

Curled-Over Toes

A bear can look really cute if you curl his toes over. To do this, add the contrasting footpad, as usual, then make a curved dent right across the underneath of the foot, just where his toes would start, by poking in a curved row with your needle. You may find it helpful to push the toes area forward with your fingers while you are poking, to accentuate the curve. You will have to keep working over this area

for a while until you have the desired amount of curve. Then, if you wish you could add some claws using the nose thread, as described on page 35.

Adding Toe Pads

You may like to divide the footpad into a base pad with several tiny toe pads above it. Use the same method to attach, but make all the toe pads on the foam first, so you can see that they are all the same size, then attach each one carefully and firmly. Toe pads like this can add a lot of fun and character to your bear.

Sharp Right-Angle Heel

Sometimes when you have needlefelted the leg and then bent the rest of the wool over at the bottom to make the foot, you don't get a nice sharp angle. Instead you get a gentle curve. If it is important to you to get a right angle heel with a nice sharp heel point, when you bend over the loose fibres, don't pull them tight. Instead, grab the foot fibres and just slightly push them to the back of the leg. When felted, this will give you a sharper angle, so that you have a well-defined heel.

Individual Toes And Fingers

If you want to shape each individual finger and toe, start the shaping while the piece is still only about half felted. Decide how many fingers you want, then make a dent with a row of pokes between the fingers. Work the dents down deeply, while felting the resulting fingers at the same time to make them firm. If one finger turns out shorter than the others, take another tiny wad of wool, felt it down a little on your foam, then felt it to the end of the short finger and continue working until it is firm and the same size as the others.

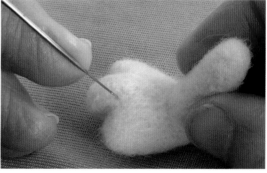

Dropped Paws

You may like to experiment with the shape of your teddybear arms. By putting another bend in the arm just under the wrist, you can make the arm with a 'dropped' paw. You can then add a contrasting pawpad underneath the paw. This tends to give a very appealing look to your bear. In the photo to the right you can just see the yellow pawpad peeping out from under the bumblebee bear's arm.

Sideways Paws

Sometimes a bear can look interesting if his arms are made so that he is leaning back on them, and they are resting on the ground. To do this, make the arms straight just like the legs, with no elbow bend in them, and then turn the paw at right angles as if it was a foot, then work the loose paw fibres back to a nice paw shape.

Basically, you are just making another leg shape, but smaller, for this type of arm. When you attach the arm to the body, remember to turn the paw out sideways, not straight ahead like the foot.

Shaped Body

You can make a great variety of shapes for the bear's body. I have shown you how to make a simple egg-shape, but you may like to model your teddybear on the early vintage bears, and give him an inwards curve to his back, and a hump between his shoulders.

Work your body shape up as normal, but before it is felted too hard, begin defining the S-bend in the back, giving him a little sticking-out bottom and the all-important hump on his back. If your hump doesn't stick up far enough when the body is finished, add a small piece of wool and felt that up into the hump.

When you attach the bear's head, it will be forward of the hump and a little lower.

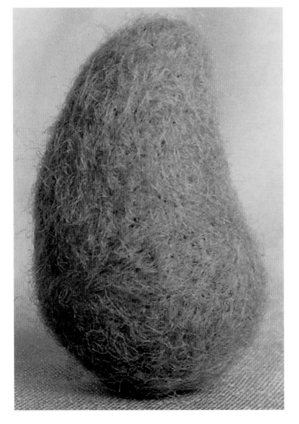

Tummy

A fat tummy can add a lot of character to a bear, so when you make the body, make it a little bit larger than you usually would, and shape it so that it is short and fat around the lower area. Add more wool if it is not fat enough, making sure you feather out the edges where the join is, so that it can't

be seen. You may like to add a tummy button; to do this simply poke your needle repeatedly into one area where his tummy button will be, and you will get a nice deep dent there.

Thread Eyebrows

Your bear's expression can benefit greatly by the simple addition of thread eyebrows. After you have inserted the eyes, stitch the eyebrows in place, coming out at the top and going in at the bottom of the eyebrow. But be aware that when you pull the stitch firm, it will be smaller than it first appeared to be. Because of the nature of the felt, the stitch will pull in slightly, so make your original stitch slightly larger than you want and only pull it in gently, to counteract this.

Adding Thick Eyebrows or Jowls

The fun thing about needlefelting is that it is so easy to add another piece on here and there for shaping. You may like to give your bear heavy protruding eyebrows, or even jowls to give him a different look. You may even like to add chubby cheeks to your bear.

When doing this, work as if you were making an ear, and felt the extra piece up on the foam first, leaving a few wispy bits of fibre sticking out where you are going to attach it to the head. Work in pairs so that you get both pieces even before you start attaching them.

Shading

You can use pencils or pens for a little gentle shading on your bear, to add character and definition. You will need to be careful how you move the pencil over the felted area, as if you are too vigorous, you will lift some of the fibres and give it a fluffy look. Areas you may like to shade are the muzzle, eyes, ears, or paws.

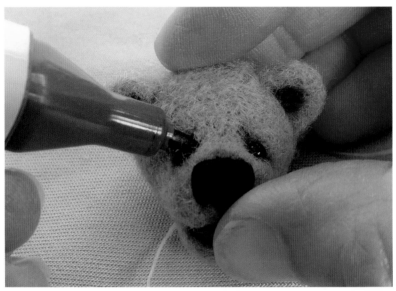

Forming A Separate Muzzle

There is another way of making a head, which you may like to try. Start by making a round ball and felting this down fairly firmly. Then pull off some more wool (the size of the muzzle will depend on the amount you pull off this time) and felt this down separately on your foam to form a cone shape, with a few wispy fibres being left at the bottom. When this is reasonably well felted down, join it to the ball that you have made, using the loose fibres to make an invisible join. The ball will form the back of the head and the cone will form the muzzle. Once the two pieces are well joined together, continue in the usual way with the detailed shaping of the face. This method can be used instead of the first method I taught you, it just depends on which you prefer.

Adding An Open Mouth

Making an open-mouth bear with needlefelting is relatively easy. Begin by making the head as you would normally, then pull off another small wad of wool which you will use to make the lower jaw. Work the shape up on your foam block as you did for your ears, making a curved shape and tucking over the wispy fibres with your felting needle to make a firm line for the edge of the jaw.

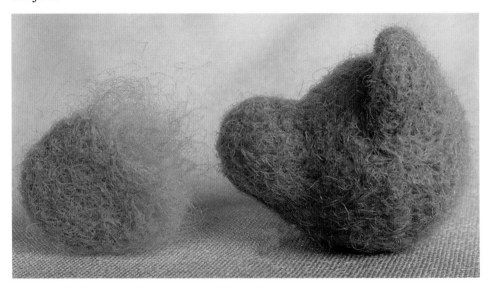

The picture above shows the bear's head and the lower jaw that we will add underneath the muzzle. Leave some wispy fibres at the base of the jaw to join on with later. You may like to add a tongue or shading to the jaw at this stage, before you join it onto the head.

When you are happy that the jaw is as firmly felted as the head, place the jaw under the bear's muzzle and position it so that it looks a nice shape, then felt in the loose fibres at the back to attach it. Make sure the jaw does not stick out as far as the muzzle, or your bear will not look nice. It must be tucked back a little from the front of the muzzle. You will need to work forward along each side of the mouth to stop the mouth gaping open when you let go, but don't needle felt too far forward or you will end up with a mouth that is closed up. Also you will be able to shape the jaw a little as you felt, to make sure that it looks even from the front.

The picture to the right shows the jaw pinned in position before it has been felted on. You can still see the wispy fibres at the back of the jaw.

The pictures below show the jaw after it has been firmly needlefelted on, both front and side view, and the finished bear's head.

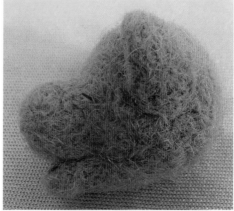

Making A Panda

Pandas are very popular little bears, and you may like to try a needlefelted panda.

The head is made in the same way as you would any head, but you have to be a bit more careful with the ears, as they are a different colour to the rest of the head, and you want a clean

straight join line where the two colours meet. To make the ears, felt them down carefully until they are almost the size you want them to be when finished on the bear's head. Leave almost no wispy ends at the base of the ear, as these will be too hard to felt in invisibly. When you have both ears felted down and ready to put on, attach them as before, but be very careful to felt it tidily, so there are no stray colours where they shouldn't be.

A panda has dark eye patches, and felting is an ideal way to show these. Make two matching oval or teardrop shapes with your contrast wool. When you have chosen your eye placement and made the eye dents, then felt on the patches firmly just before you insert the eyes.

The panda's body is in two colours, and the best way to do this is to make the lower part of the body first, felt it up to the completed stage, leaving the upper part where the contrast colour will go, as a flattish surface with possibly a few wisps (not much) sticking out.

Now use your contrast colour to felt up a cone shape, which will be the upper part of the panda's body. Don't make it too large, or your panda will appear elongated, and remember to leave just a few wisps of fibre sticking out at the lower end. When the cone is nearly felted

down, add it to the body. Poke the needle all around the edges, going in a downwards motion, but also in an upwards motion, so that you are taking fibres from the lower body up into the new piece, and also the other way around. Poke the needle quite a few times from the neck area down into the centre of the body as well. It is very important

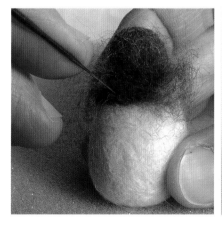

to make a strong bond here, and try to make a nice clean line where the two colours join.

If you find that you have an indent where the two colours meet, simply take a little extra wool and wrap it around the body at that point. Needlefelt it in place, making sure that you don't end up with a visible circle of fibres going around the body. Try to mix up the directions of the fibres before you apply this wool.

The legs and arms are made in the normal way, but because they are normally a dark colour on a panda, they may benefit from the addition of contrasting pawpads, as discussed earlier. You could use the same colour as already used for the lower body and head, or add a completely new colour, if preferred. For instance, you could jazz up a black and white panda with pink or lilac pawpads, and then add a little of the same colour to the inside of his ears to match.

Accessories

You may like to add needlefelted accessories to your teddybears. Using the same techniques as I have already shown, it is possible to make all sorts of little extra pieces that your bears can hold, or wear, or that can be placed beside them.

Various clothing and hats are the obvious choices, but your bear may like a little companion, or a ball or 'wooden' block to hold. You may like to make a fairy bear with needlefelted wand and wings, or create a woodland fantasy scene with some toadstools, large leaves for them to sit in, and so on.

The picture below shows just some of the possibilities that you could make, and I am sure your imagination will help you to come up with many more ideas. The little gingerbread man could be swapped for a tiny gollywog or doll, or even another miniature bear, for a larger bear to hold. The tiny rat was made as a companion for a bear called 'The Pied Piper'.

Needlefelting Supplies

As supplies for needlefelting may not readily be found in shops in your area at the moment, I have available just about everything you may need, from needles, wool and foam blocks, to eyes, dental floss and nose thread.

Needles: a variety of sizes from 36 to 42.

Wool Roving: (sliver) comes in many colours, from natural to very bright colours. I stock corriedale and merino wool in small bags, which should be enough to make two to four bears, depending on size.

Foam Blocks: cut into 15 cm (5 inch) squares, or larger if preferred.

Eyes: 3 mm German glass eyes on a wire shank, also some small black onyx bead eyes, which are totally round with a hole through the middle for stitching, ideal for very tiny bears.

Dental Floss and **Nose Thread** by the metre if you prefer not to buy a whole roll.

Beginner's Pack: Kits that contain all you need to make your first needlefelted teddybear.

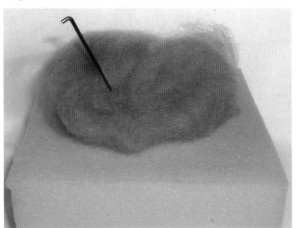

You will find a complete **list of supplies** on the needlefelting page of my website, **www.cobwebcottage.co.nz** or you can write to me at:
233 Kereone Road, R D 1, Morrinsville, New Zealand.
I am happy to post around the world.

Summary

I do hope you have enjoyed working through this book, and that the techniques and tips that I have shown you have encouraged you to stretch your own creative imagination, so that you feel confident to create your own little works of art. You do not have to make only teddybears. There is no limit to the possibilities of needlefelting; imagine dogs, bunnies, elephants, pixies and toadstools, to name but a few. There are no rules for needlefelting either; if something works for you and you like it, then do it. As you practice, each piece you make will turn out better than the one before. As you become more skilled and confident with felting you will find that you have more control over the final outcome of the piece you are creating.

Happy felting!

About The Author

I have been a teddybear artist since 1999, selling my Cobweb Cottage miniature bears mainly on the internet, where they have found homes in England, USA, Canada, Europe, Australia, and Japan, as well as in New Zealand. I have also attended many teddybear shows in NZ. My bears are usually made from vintage velvet, plus the occasional mohair bear, and now I make quite a few needlefelted miniature bears as well, which are usually displayed on my website.

I was first introduced to needlefelting in 2002 and find it a fascinating way to create beautiful teddybears. At the time I had not heard of anyone else in New Zealand who was doing needlefelting in this manner, so I began teaching others, and this has led to a great interest in the subject. All of the bears that you have seen in this book have been made by me, and many of them have been sold on my website, www.cobwebcottage.co.nz.

I am now teaching needlefelting through workshops, where I offer a beginner kitset, also supplies and this booklet, so that people can refer back afterwards to what I have taught them. If anyone is interested in attending one of my workshops, you can contact me through my website, or at the address on the Supplies page of this book.

I am sure you will enjoy this book and I wish you many happy hours of needlefelting!

Barbara Allen